the

(73)

Sayings of Light, Power, and Wisdom

Undrai Fizer

DIVINE H HOUSE
B O O K S

ISBN_978-0-692-65875-8

As YOU begin your day, or even close your evening, "remember" that You've already won. Every now and then it's good to have a few "thought sparks" in our possession. Thought-Sparks are simple, yet profound sayings that generate within us some sort of "spiritual momentum and rejuvenation." We really don't need much; just that little something to feed our already, prospering Journey. In my book, *"The 365; A Personal Compass to Self-Discovery & Enlightenment"* 2013 Divine House Books), YOU will find a collection of sayings, affirmations, and power quotes that do just that. Think of this book as the different side of The 365, as well as the companion to *"The Excuse-less Life, 34 Inner-laws for Living Above Distraction"* (2015 Divine House Books).

Life becomes more powerful and clearer as YOU pay attention to the details of it. Vision and Enlightenment will "open your

eyes" to the Soul of LIFE and allow YOU
to walk your Path in confidence and power!
Hopefully, the words of this book will aid
in your SEEING capacity. There is so much
more of LIFE and Spirit to enjoy within
yourself. Give yourself a chance to SEE
"what YOU will happen to!"

Enjoy…

TO MY FAMILY,
We will always have one another
through every Shift in Life...
To all of my family in Spirit,
We will always have one another
through every Shift in Life...

NOTHINGNESS

can creep in easily by way of

toleration. Before YOU know it

TIME will pass and we'll

still be "here!"

GET UP EARLY and YOU

won't have to rush! Casual

pursuits of dreams and visions will

leave YOU empty handed, even

though you've "tried!"

*We are spirits that are
already "Beautiful" in the eyes
of God. But when our MINDS
experience the love of God
"our lives will follow!"*

Are YOU seeking the best for YOU,

or the most convenient for YOU?

Your truth, whatever it may be, will

determine your "pace!"

What are YOU expecting

today? Imagine accordingly!

Do accordingly!

*Master obeying the "inner-laws
and simple directives" that are always
flowing in your silent soul. YOU will
hear those frequencies more than
YOU hear an "audible command!"
These frequencies lead to greater
AWAKENINGS and Openness!*

THIS IS YOUR WEEK

to do something incredibly new,

nervous, and necessary!

The Excitement of New Beginnings

and Thought will make YOU "scared"

with Delight! Unfamiliar Paths carry

an exuberance within them!

YES!! You want to attract those who will place great demands upon your ability! Both of YOU will increase because of it!

Create an opportunity for every gift that YOU possess and flow with. For every talent, create a Door. LIFE is not meant to be a toil for YOU!

When exploring your vision
"YOU will receive, as a reward, the
degree of which you're willing to
exchange!" Whatever YOU give up
for the LOVE of your LIFE, to this
degree YOU will receive!

NOW has arrived! Prepare yourself to do something bigger than your convenience. Put yourself out there! MOVE BEYOND "the easy!"

Your wealth is hidden within the

Greater Responsibilities and Details

that YOU find "overwhelming!"

There is no "safe way" to do FAITH!

There's only trust. After You've done

all you can do, LET GO and FLY!

Never hold yourself back, waiting on

permission from others to "let YOU

go!" What is it that is calling

after YOU?

If You can do without it, YOU will

never go after it. If it's not calling

your name "you'll never listen

for its opportunity!

Beliefs, without BECOMING, are

but mere acknowledgments

of information!

*Your life, loves, pursuits, values,
disciplines, and persistence naturally
reveal what YOU "believe in!"*

Your LIFE will go as far as

YOU love it!

God "found" me through Me. I was never really "lost." I simply couldn't "see, feel, or touch," who I really was. Within YOU is the LIGHT!

No matter where YOU are, LOVE is always thinking of YOU, and it is always seeking YOU out to rescue YOU from the "fears" of Self!

If YOU don't need "IT" you'll

never see "IT!" What is it that

YOU "need?"

Listen to the NOW and "The Rhythm!" Don't allow "what has always been," to blind YOU from the "Sound of NOW!"

YOU may look like you're attached

to "nothing," but really, YOU ARE!

YOU are attached to an eternal

rhythm that is re-planting YOU

to something NEW!

*You're not in "limbo." You're in the
middle of a SHIFT that is touching
every area of your life in both the
physical and the spiritual!*

Follow your heart. YOU already

know when it's pure and when it's

questionable. YOU really don't

have to ask!

Live "like YOU know what YOU want!" When YOU know what YOU deserve, what YOU desire will obey your VOICE!

YOU will always quit "if"

YOU don't feel that you're worth

the persistence or the trouble!

YOU must go on "for YOU!"

*We are the reflections of what
we've given our lives to and for! We
are the reflections of our motives.
Give yourself to something happy!*

"TODAY" desires to agree with your Intentions. It wants to create with YOU, for YOU, and through YOU! Today says that YOU are on its Mind!

*YOU are the "first person"
that follows your leadership! Lead
Yourself well and the
Atmosphere will notice. Fail, and
distractions will!*

In this Journey, if YOU don't get anything else, Please do not take your TIME for granted! Don't give it away to any and every "thing!"

When your Soul is true it will

make sure YOU can find confidence

in IT first before YOU look for it in

another. There is no need for

YOU to wander!

We are the Image of God.

There is nothing else greater for

Him to do!

If YOU don't think your soul

is beautiful "you'll never follow it

anywhere!"

You're simply going to have to trust that you're good enough. It can be a pain when you're used to getting permission from others to do that!

Never trust the views

of a "quitter!"

YOU cannot draw to your life

anything you're not passionate about.

Everything that comes to YOU must

already see itself in YOU!

If YOU won't live for it

"YOU will not die for it!"

"UGLY" is not a look, it's an attitude! Smart is not a test score, it's an attitude. EVERYTHING is an attitude! Got it?

Why would YOU hold yourself

back from everything good that

YOU are? What are YOU afraid of?

Be Beautiful, Bold, and Present!

God spoke to all of us, before the

world began. His love is reminding

YOU daily of The Conversation!

You're more than YOU think

YOU are!

Be confident. When YOU are overcome with happiness "stop looking for disaster!" Love is eternal "when YOU allow it to be!"

Love "is" God, even in strange places.

Wherever there is TRUTH, there is

love. Where there is LOVE, there is

the Presence of God!

When YOU tell yourself that you're

going to do better, LISTEN!

Create as God would create. If YOU feel that you're a "liar" YOU will never speak your voice. Truth creates a Harvest, always!

Miracles are the byproducts of one's movement beyond fear, the mundane, and the common!

Freedom within everything

YOU are confirms the Love and

Power of God!

When God has been truly realized,

"Freedom Arises!"

Success comes to those who are as committed to the Lesson in their free time as they were in the classroom!

Every Place is Yours already. But in the fullness of TIME "you will be invited without measure!"

Never cry over the loss of parasite!

(That's what my friend Dee said.)

Create tomorrow, TODAY!

Your GIFT will motivate the Universe to expand itself for YOU in order for YOU to have room to spread your wings! Do something with YOU!

Walk wisely. Don't "shut your doors"

before they get a chance to open!

Changes in the world will come as a result of fantasizing on responsibility instead of irresponsible pleasure!

The *"Demands"* on your LIFE will

determine *"the Flow"* of your Life.

Wasted time are from

"wasted demands!"

Discern when it's Time for YOU to

leave and where YOU are led to go!

YOU cannot control the storms and

wars "in other folks" mind!

Remain in your peace.

God will "use" YOU "in spite of

YOU!" We don't "scare" God.

We "scare" ourselves!

Sometimes, YOU will have to remind yourself that you're doing an awesome job! YOU MAKE LIFE GOOD!

We will quickly invest in the people

or things we desire to imitate most!

We love to give to "what we may also

become!" Think about it!

Your happiness isn't making

everybody happy. You don't have to

tone it down. Just tone it elsewhere.

Keep the "TONE!"

When YOU "know" what YOU

want, the things YOU DO NOT

WANT "won't be done!" You will

get "what YOU do!"

When YOU celebrate yourself "the

lack of it from another" will

never stop YOU!

YOU were created with a YES already

established within YOU! You don't

have to wait! Flow NOW!

Could it be that we are afraid of true commitment out of fear of losing our "flexibility of freedom and its many curves and angles?"

Don't make excuses to remain in the dark "when LIGHT is available!"

The Hand of Abundance is in your

house. Stop trying to remember that

you're "broke!" Stir up your Mind.

Kiss the Hand that flows!

Every creative idea must awaken

a Passion within YOU "in order

for Manifestation to arrive!"

Dead "inspiration" will only

create sadness!

When your "room" gets small

enough, you'll probably get out of

there. Until then, you'll tolerate

the lack.

Don't destroy a beautiful friendship

with yourself "for the sake of not

having enemies, haters, or people

being offended with YOU!"

Purpose does not reveal itself to

be walked away from! When

you're ready to live it out it

will reveal itself!

www.ingramcontent.com/pod-product-compliance
Lightning Source LLC
Chambersburg PA
CBHW061156040426
42445CB00013B/1697